The Magic School Bus® PRESENTS
The Human Body

Scholastic Inc.

Previous page: X-ray of the chest

Photos © 2014: Alamy Images: 10, 28 bottom right (Science Photo Library), 15, 29 bottom right (Tetra Images); Dreamstime: 12 right (Alon Othnay), 9 top right (Landd09), 7 (Lenalir), 18 left, 29 top right (Spfotocz); Fotolia/ Light Impression: 12 left, 29 top left; Getty Images: 3 center, 14 left (Adriana Varela Photography), 19 (Jamie Grill/Tetra images RF), 4 top left (Stocktrek Images), 6 top left (Tim Ridley/Dorling Kindersley); Media Bakery: 31 right (Guy Cali/Corbis), 27 (Kris Timken); Science Source: 4 background, 5 (3D4Medical), 3 top, 8 right, 28 top left (AJPhoto), 20 (Alfred Pasieka), 24 left, 28 bottom left (Biophoto Associates), 30 (Blair Seitz), 21 right (David M. Phillips), 3 bottom, 22 background, 23, 28 top right (David Mack), 22 top left (José Antonio Peñas), 13 (Pasieka), 26 left (Roger Harris), 1, 8 left (Scott Camazine), 21 left (SPL), 16 left (Steve Gschmeissner), 25 (Susumu Nishinaga), 11 top right (Science Source); Shutterstock, Inc.: cover background (dream designs), cover (Kozorez Vladislav); Superstock, Inc./CHASSENET/BSIP: 31 left; Thinkstock/b.d.s: 17, 29 bottom left.

ISBN 978-0-545-68364-7

Produced by Potomac Global Media, LLC

All text, illustrations, and compilations © 2014 Scholastic Inc.
Based on The Magic School Bus series © Joanna Cole and Bruce Degen
Text by Dan Green Illustrations by Carolyn Bracken
Consultant: Francesca Norris, Ph.D. Biomedical imaging

Published by Scholastic Inc., 557 Broadway, New York, NY 10012.

16 15   21 22/0

Cover design by Paul Banks
Interior design by Thomas Keenes
Photo research by Sharon Southren

Printed in the U.S.A.   40
First printing, July 2014

Contents

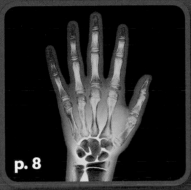

p. 8

p. 14

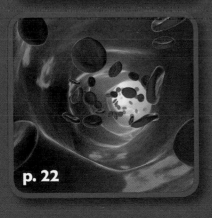

p. 22

Inside a Cell

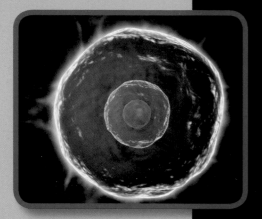

The human body is made up of tiny cells like this one. The body grows by adding new cells.

I t was time for science in Ms. Frizzle's class and we were watching a movie about the human body. The Friz explained that our bodies are made up of billions of tiny building blocks called cells. "Hop on the bus and I'll show you," she told us. A moment later, we zoomed right into the film.

Different types of cells build different body parts. We have blood cells, brain cells, muscle cells, and many more.

Cell makeup

Each cell has smaller parts inside, which bring food in, take waste out, and help protect the cell.

Cells rock!

What is a cell?
by Wanda

All living things are made up of cells. Although they vary in size, all cells are smaller than the human eye can see. Each one contains all the equipment needed to keep an animal, plant, or bacteria alive. Cells divide to make new copies of themselves and this is how bodies grow. Each human starts out as just one cell but grows into a body with thousands of billions of cells.

Self-contained unit

A cell is like a watery bag. Its flexible wall keeps all of the parts of the cell safe inside.

Energy to burn

The parts of the cell that produce the energy a cell needs are called mitochondria. Each tiny cell has thousands of them.

Control center

At the heart of each cell is the nucleus. It directs all the action in the cell.

Frizzle Fact

It takes a mind-blowing number of cells to make a human body. The average body contains about ten trillion cells — that's a thousand billion!

Skin, Hair, and Nails

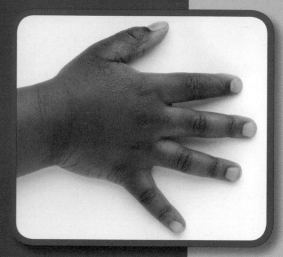

Skin is the body's outer covering. It keeps the insides together in a human-shaped package, and protects the body from the world outside. It's smooth . . . and almost entirely covered in fine hairs that are often too tiny to see! Hair grows out of nearly every part of the skin.

Nails protect the ends of the fingers and toes. They are useful for scratching and gripping hard things.

Under the Skin

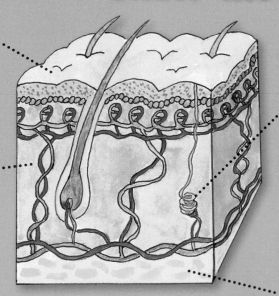

Outer protection
Skin has three layers. The top layer forms a protective barrier for the body.

Sweat gland
These tiny glands release sweat onto the surface of the skin through pores.

Nerve center
The middle layer is full of nerve cells that sense hot, cold, and touch.

Fatty layer
The deepest part of the skin stores a layer of fat. This protects the body from injury and keeps it warm.

Frizzle Fact
All of the skin cells at the surface of the skin are dead. In one year, an adult sheds about 8 pounds (3.6 kilograms) of old skin.

Hair grows from special pits under the skin's surface, called follicles.

Hair and nails are made out of the same material, called keratin.

Here's the skinny on skin!

Let it grow

Hair grows at about half an inch (1.25 centimeters) a month. Nails grow more slowly, at about ⅛ inch (3 millimeters) a month.

Human skin
by Arnold

Skin provides a stretchy, waterproof outer wrapper for the human body. Skin's protective barrier keeps germs out of the body, and can regrow when it gets broken or cut. It also helps keep a person cool by producing sweat from glands when the body gets hot. The thickest layer of skin is on the soles of the feet, while the eyelids have the thinnest skin.

Bones and Muscles

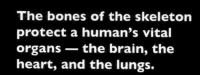

The bones of the skeleton protect a human's vital organs — the brain, the heart, and the lungs.

X-ray vision
Doctors often use X-rays to see inside the body. An X-ray can show where a bone is broken.

It's alive!
The body's bones aren't dead, dry, and crumbly, like bones in museums. They are alive and grow new cells just like other parts of the body.

Frizzle Fact
The body's largest bone is the femur, or thigh bone. The smallest bone is the stirrup bone in the ear.

Bones connect to make the skeleton, which supports the body's weight and keeps it upright. The skeleton bends at the joints to move the bones. Muscles pull on the bones to allow the body to do amazing things, such as writing or riding a bike.

Each muscle pulls in one direction. Muscles work in pairs to move joints, such as elbows. One muscle pulls while the other relaxes.

Let's bone up on this!

Inside a Joint

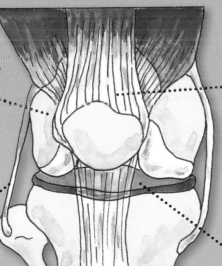

Joint
Bones come together at joints. Most joints move so the body can change position.

Tendon
Tough fibers called tendons attach muscles to the bones of the joint.

Ligament
Strong cords called ligaments join bones to other bones and help strengthen joints.

Soft cushion
Bouncy pads made of a material called cartilage cushion the joint as the body moves.

All about bones
by Keesha

Bones are made of a hard mineral called calcium phosphate. Eating calcium-rich foods, like milk and cheese, can help build them up and make them strong. Adult humans have 206 bones in their bodies, while babies have 270. This is because some of the bones in the skull and back join up as a child grows bigger. More than half of all the bones in the human body are found in the hands and the feet.

Brain

Making connections
Nerves carry information about the outside world to the brain.

The cerebrum
The biggest part of the brain is called the cerebrum. Different parts of the cerebrum deal with different body functions.

Brain stem
This part of the brain controls automatic processes like breathing, digesting, and the beating heart.

I hope I'm not getting on his nerves!

Frizzle Fact
The brain uses one-fifth of the energy the body takes from food!

The brain controls everything a person does. Some things, like breathing and digestion, happen automatically. Other things, like choosing what to wear, need to be thought out. The brain receives information from all over the body. It makes sense of that information and returns signals to different body parts, telling them how to react.

EYES OPEN   EYES CLOSED

Scientists use scans to observe brain function. They can see what happens, for example, when the eyes are open or closed.

I've got brains on my mind!

Brain Map

Making decisions
The frontal lobe controls forward planning.

Touch
The parietal lobe processes information relating to touch.

Sight
The occipital lobe handles vision.

Memory and sound
The temporal lobes handle long-term memory.

Movement
The cerebellum controls body movement and balance.

How does the brain work?
by Tim

The brain is the body's third largest organ (after the skin and the liver). It is like a giant network, with billions and billions of tiny nerve cells carrying information from one part of the brain to another. Learning how to do new things makes new nerve cells, and the more the brain practices doing something, the quicker the connections get.

Nervous System and Senses

Nerve endings near the surface of the tongue tell the brain whether something you are eating is hot or cold.

Nerves are like cables. They are made up of nerve cells that send signals to one another. A bundle of nerves called the spinal cord runs up the center of the back. It is well-protected by the bones of the spine. The spinal cord leads directly into the brain and constantly zips messages to and from the brain and other parts of the body.

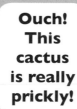

Ouch! This cactus is really prickly!

Nerve signals can travel at 180 miles (290 kilometers) per hour!

Touch sensors in your skin tell you right away when something is prickly so you can move away from danger fast.

Mission control

The brain uses the nervous system to send out instructions to the body. It closely monitors all incoming signals.

Two-way traffic

Nerves send information to the brain along the spinal cord, and signals travel back down the cord from the brain.

It all makes sense!

The Senses

By Dorothy Ann

The senses help you understand the world. There are five different ways of getting information. Vision lets you see the shapes of things. Hearing helps you to make sense of sound waves picked up by the ear. Smell notices chemicals in the air, while taste detects them in food and drink. Touch sensors all over your skin help you feel shapes with your hands and the wind on your face. Touch also helps you feel pain to keep you safe from hurm.

Outer limits

Some nerves send information relating to the senses. Other nerves tell the muscles when and where to move.

Eye

Sight is a very important sense in humans. The eyes are like cameras. They focus light onto special cells inside them. Then they work together to make a clear, three-dimensional picture of what they see. The brain processes this picture so you know what you are looking at.

Newborn babies make crying sounds, but their eyes don't produce tears until they are at least four weeks old.

Mini Camera

My eyes use lenses to focus light, just like this telescope!

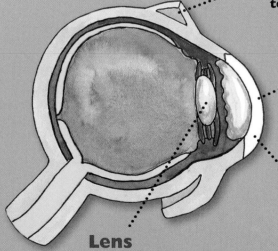

Directional control
Muscles pull on the eyeball to point it toward a subject.

Iris
The muscular iris gets bigger or smaller to control the amount of light let in by the pupil.

Pupil
The pupil is a hole at the front of the eye. It lets light in.

Lens
The lens focuses incoming light onto light-sensitive cells on the eye's back wall.

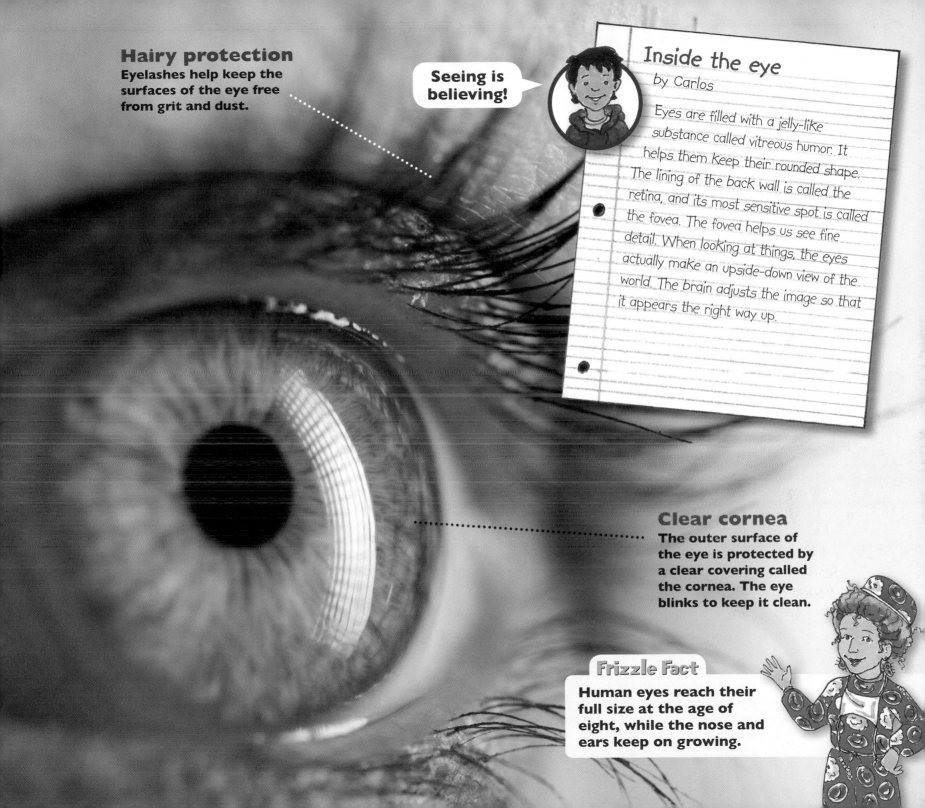

Hairy protection
Eyelashes help keep the surfaces of the eye free from grit and dust.

Seeing is believing!

Inside the eye
by Carlos

Eyes are filled with a jelly-like substance called vitreous humor. It helps them keep their rounded shape. The lining of the back wall is called the retina, and its most sensitive spot is called the fovea. The fovea helps us see fine detail. When looking at things, the eyes actually make an upside-down view of the world. The brain adjusts the image so that it appears the right way up.

Clear cornea
The outer surface of the eye is protected by a clear covering called the cornea. The eye blinks to keep it clean.

Frizzle Fact
Human eyes reach their full size at the age of eight, while the nose and ears keep on growing.

Ear

The ears pick up on the smallest vibrations in the air and feed the sounds through to the brain. Each ear has three zones, and each zone deals with a different part of the hearing process. The ears are also important for balancing the body on two legs and keeping it from falling over.

Good Vibrations

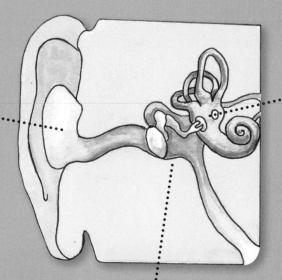

Microscopic hair cells inside the inner ear detect sounds. They trigger nerve signals that then travel to the brain.

Outer ear
The outer ear collects sound from the world outside and sends it down the ear canal.

Inner ear
This curly tube is filled with fluid. Tiny hair cells pick up movements of the fluid and the brain hears this as sound.

Middle ear
Sounds make the eardrum vibrate. Three small bones transfer the vibrations to the inner ear.

Frizzle Fact

The three smallest bones in the body are all found in the ear. They are called the malleus, incus, and stirrup bones.

Ear flap
The outer ear is the only part that other humans can see. Most of the ear lies inside the head.

Loud noise can damage your hearing.

So let's stop shouting!

I'm well-balanced!

Having good balance
by Phoebe

The ears help people balance. Just above the inner ear are three small loops filled with liquid. When the body moves around, the liquid sloshes back and forth, triggering tiny hair cells that send nerve signals back to the brain. These signals help a person keep track of their position. They also allow the body to do amazing feats of balance, such as walking, bending over, and doing handstands.

Earhole
The ear canal is part of the outer ear. It is self-cleaning and produces a thick earwax to mop up any dirt that gets into the tube.

Mouth and Nose

The mouth is the first stop on the journey food takes through the body. The teeth mash it with saliva to break it down. Taste buds on the tongue taste the food. Receptors inside the nose detect aromas in the food, which makes the taste even stronger. This is the start of the process of digestion.

Air is breathed in and out of the nose through two nostrils.

Your body makes more than 2 pints (1 liter) of saliva every day!

That's a lot of spit!

A Tooth

Molars
Molars are teeth at the back of the mouth that grind and mash food.

Enamel
A hard enamel coating toughens teeth against wear and tear.

Pulp
The soft core of a tooth contains blood vessels and nerves.

Dentin
Dentin is hard, like bone, but not as hard as enamel. Most of a tooth is made of dentin.

Teeth

Children have about 20 milk teeth or baby teeth. They all fall out, to be replaced by permanent adult teeth.

Taste buds

Tiny taste buds on the tongue send taste sensations to the brain when the mouth is busy chewing solid food and drinking liquids.

A very tasteful topic!

All about the tongue
by Ralphie

Did you know that your tongue is a muscle? Well, it's actually a bunch of muscles attached to the back of the mouth. A flap of skin called the frenulum makes sure that it doesn't flop backward down the throat. The tongue is a multipurpose device, useful for licking ice cream, singing, talking, and digging bits of food out of teeth! The tongue has between 3,000 and 10,000 taste buds, which are replaced nearly every two weeks. That sure keeps everything tasting fresh!

Frizzle Fact

Most adults have 32 teeth, but some toothy record-breakers have had as many as 35 teeth!

Digestive System

Stomach
Chemicals in the stomach break down food. Strong muscles in the stomach wall help by churning the food around.

Small intestine
The broken-down food mixture spends around four hours in the small intestine.

Large intestine
The large intestine absorbs the water left in the food mixture. As it does so, anything that is left over forms waste.

You can't digest gum, but it doesn't stick in your belly forever — it ends up in your waste!

Rectum
The waste is stored here, ready to exit the body.

F ood goes on a fantastic journey through the human body. It starts the moment anything is consumed, and involves the mouth, the stomach, and the intestines. By the time the food reaches the rectum, it will have traveled as far as 29½ feet (9 meters), releasing all its goodness into the body.

Digestion: How it works
by Wanda

Digestion begins when food is chewed, mixes with saliva, and is swallowed. In the stomach, it is broken apart by a combination of strong acid and digestive chemicals. The mixture that is made in the process empties out into the small intestine. The small intestine extracts nutrients from the mixture   with the help of digestive juices made by the liver and pancreas. The large intestine recycles water.

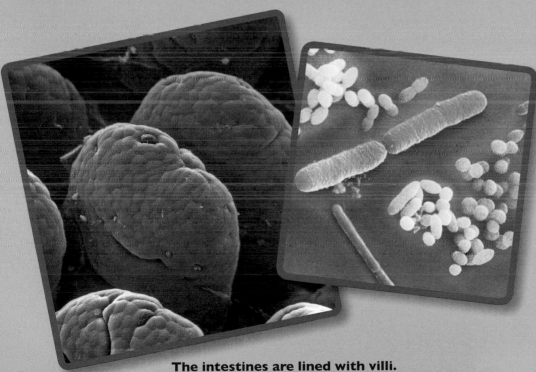

The intestines are lined with villi. These look like tiny fingers. With huge surface areas, the villi absorb nutrients into the bloodstream.

The intestines are full of friendly bacteria that help break down food.

Frizzle Fact

An adult's small intestine is almost 23 feet (7 meters) long — that's about as long as our school bus!

Blood and Circulation

Blood is like an express delivery service for the body. It is pumped around by the heart and carries oxygen from the lungs and nutrients from the intestines directly to the body's cells. Then the blood returns to the heart, taking carbon dioxide gas back to the lungs, where it is breathed out. Other waste products pass through the kidneys for disposal.

Blood contains specialized white blood cells, pictured above. These cells protect the body from germs and help fight infections.

Red blood cells contain an iron-rich chemical called hemoglobin. This chemical absorbs oxygen in the lungs.

Go with the flow
The watery part of blood is called plasma. It keeps the blood flowing inside small blood vessels.

Frizzle Fact

Blood speeds around the body — after leaving the heart, only a minute passes before the blood has returned.

Your body makes 17 million red bloods cells every second!

Circulation city!

The red stuff
Red blood cells carrying oxygen in the arteries look bright red. They turn a darker red in the veins, once they have delivered oxygen to the body's cells.

The Bloodstream
by Arnold

The bloodstream is also known as the circulatory system. It connects the body from head to toe. Except for hair and nails, there isn't a single part of the body it doesn't reach. All blood passes through the heart on its journey around the body. Arteries carry blood away from the heart, while veins carry blood toward the heart. Smaller blood vessels are called capillaries.

Heart and Lungs

These organs work tirelessly to keep the human body alive. The heart pumps hard for its whole life, never once taking a break! The lungs breathe in life-giving oxygen, which powers chemical reactions in the body. When the lungs breathe out again, they expel carbon dioxide into the air.

The lungs contain an amazing 1,500 miles (2,400 kilometers) of airways.

Heart and Lungs

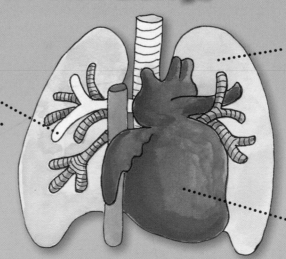

Alveoli
The lung's airways end in tiny sacs called alveoli.

The lungs
The lungs draw air into the body from outside. With every breath, the body takes in 1 pint (0.5 liters) of air.

Beating heart
The heart sits between the lungs, pointing slightly to the left.

Frizzle Fact

When resting, adults breathe more slowly than babies. A baby takes around 40 breaths a minute, while an adult takes as few as 12.

Heart valve
Valves in the heart control the blood flow between the four chambers.

A resting heart beats between 60 and 100 times a minute.

I ♥ my heart!

How the heart works
by Keesha

The heart is a muscle about the size of a clenched fist. It sits in the center of the body. Inside are four chambers — the top two are called atria and the bottom two are the ventricles. Blood is pumped into the atria first, then into the ventricles, and finally back out into the body. When you listen to someone's heartbeat, the double BA-BOOM you hear is the snapping shut of the valves between the chambers after the blood has left.

Heartstrings
Blood flows through the four chambers of the heart, passing through one-way valves. The heartstrings make sure the valves stay closed.

Taking Care of Your Body

Everyone loves to feel strong, fit, and healthy. Like any machine, the human body needs to be looked after to make sure it runs well and lasts for a long time. Eating the right kinds of foods and exercising regularly will make the body feel good and grow up strong. Keeping clean helps the body beat germs.

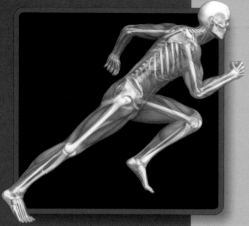

Exercising makes the muscles and bones grow stronger.

Brush your teeth twice a day to keep tooth decay at bay.

My Plate

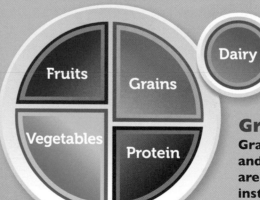

Dairy foods
Calcium-rich dairy foods, such as milk, yogurt, and cheese, help keep bones healthy.

Fruits
Fruits provide your body with essential nutrients, such as vitamin C.

Grains
Grains include bread, rice, and pasta. Whole grains are best, so try brown rice instead of white.

Vegetables
Vegetables are loaded with fiber, minerals, and vitamins.

Protein
Protein comes from meat, fish, and beans. It helps build healthy muscles.

Let's move!
An hour of outdoor play each day is fun and it's good for your body!

I'm fit. Are you?

Healthy living
by Tim

The body needs a regular supply of healthy food to provide it with fuel to burn. It also needs enough water to keep things running smoothly. Don't forget that you only get one set of adult teeth. Careful brushing after eating will keep them strong enough for a lifetime. Wash your hands before meals and after going to the bathroom. And remember, human bodies need enough sleep at night to recharge their batteries.

Be a fit kid
A fit body is one that does the things it is asked to do. Being active; limiting time spent on the computer, watching TV, or playing video games; and trying new foods are great ways to make a start.

Frizzle Fact
Doctors recommend that children get 10 to 11 hours of sleep each night.

Incredible Body Facts

Amazing bones

Bone cells are replaced and renewed all the time so that each person receives a new skeleton every ten years or so. The hyoid bone, in the back of the throat, is the only bone in the body that's not connected to another one. Human thighbones are stronger than concrete.

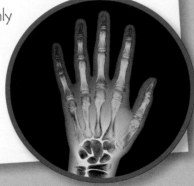

Bloodstream basics

There are about 6 quarts (5.6 liters) of blood in the body. Pumped around the body, it travels nearly 12,000 miles (19,300 kilometers) in a day. Joined together end to end, the blood vessels would stretch around the world nearly 2½ times!

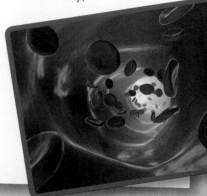

Incredible lungs

Over 30,000 tiny tubes called bronchioles are squeezed inside human lungs. These help the lungs to breathe in around 2,900 gallons (11,000 liters) of air every day. The left lung is smaller than the right lung to leave room under the rib cage for the heart.

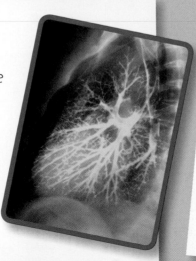

Brain benders

The brain has 100 billion neurons (message-carrying nerve cells), but loses around 85,000 brain cells every day. The average person has 70,000 thoughts a day. An adult's brain weighs around 3 pounds (1.5 kilograms). The brain uses as much as 20 percent of a person's energy.

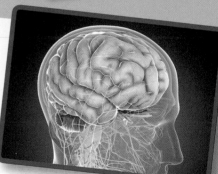

Well done, class!
I hope you can join me
on our next adventure!

Taste sensations

The sense of taste is less acute than the other senses. The tongue detects just five tastes — sweet, sour, salty, bitter, and savory. The more taste buds you have, the better your sense of taste. An adult has an average of 9,000 taste buds on his or her tongue.

The sense of smell

The human nose is so sensitive it can pick out more than 10,000 different smells. The smell center is a thumbnail-sized patch located high up in the nasal passage. It contains six million special smelling cells. That's nothing compared to a dog's 220 million smell cells.

Inside the ear

Ears use earwax to keep them clean. It catches dust and dirt that drifts in from the outside world and pushes it back out of the ear. The inner ear is about the size of a pencil eraser and is crammed with 20,000 hairs. Kids are able to hear more higher-pitched sounds than adults.

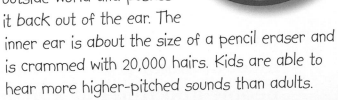

Sharp eyes

An eye weighs about 1 ounce (25 grams), which is the same as ten pennies. Every blink takes about one-tenth of a second, and humans blink about four million times a year! All babies are color-blind when they are born. Fully developed eyes can see around 500 different shades of gray!

Body Experts

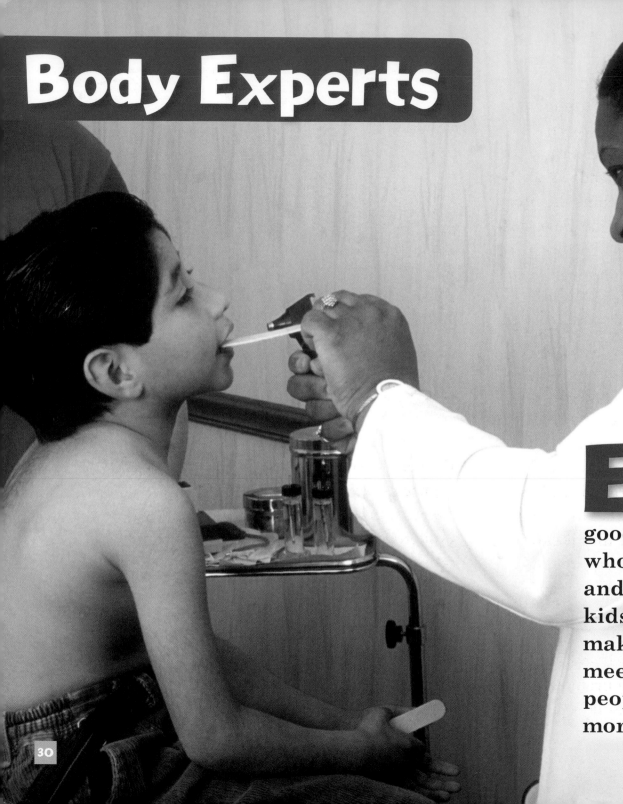

Everybody gets sick sometimes. It's not nice feeling ill, but there is good news — there are people who are specially trained, and whose job it is to help kids through problems and make them better. Let's meet some of these amazing people and find out a little more about what they do.

❮ Pediatrician

Pediatricians are doctors who specialize in helping children of all ages, from newborn babies to teenagers. Children are constantly growing and so have age-specific needs as well as general health issues. Pediatricians monitor a child's height and weight to see that he or she is healthy and growing well. These doctors also deal with a wide variety of common medical conditions, including bug bites, coughs and colds, and broken bones.

⌄ Nutritionist

Making sure you eat enough of the right types of foods is very important when you are young. Your body is growing, and what you put into it can have an impact on how your body develops and whether or not it stays healthy. Nutritionists check that you are getting just what you need. They also look into the causes of allergies to see if something in your diet lies at the root of the problem. The most common food allergies are milk, eggs, fish, nuts, and wheat.

⌃ Physical therapist

Physical therapists are trained to deal with injuries such as sprains, muscle strains, concussion (being knocked out), fractures, and broken bones. Strains come from overuse of muscles, tendons, and joints during games and training. Sometimes pain flares up during a growth spurt. This is when your body grows quickly and joints and muscles can't keep up with such rapid change. Physical therapists advise rest when necessary, and they can help you begin exercising safely again once your injury has healed.

Words to Know

Artery One of the tubes that carries blood from the heart to the rest of the body.

Bacteria Microscopic, single-celled living things that exist everywhere and can either be helpful or harmful to the body.

Chemical A compound or substance in the body.

Fiber A part of fruits, vegetables, and grains that passes through the body but is not digested. It helps food move through the intestines.

Gland An organ in the body that produces or releases natural chemicals.

Infection An illness caused by bacteria or viruses.

Kidney One of a pair of organs in the body that clean the blood by filtering out waste matter and turning it into urine.

Liver The organ in a human or animal body that cleans the blood and produces bile, which helps digest food.

Microscopic Something that is so small it cannot be seen with the human eye.

Nucleus The central part of a cell.

Retina The lining at the back of the eyeball. The retina is sensitive to light and sends images of the things you see to your brain.

Sac A pouchlike structure in a plant or animal that often contains a liquid.

Saliva The watery fluid in the mouth that keeps it moist and helps soften food for swallowing.

Taste bud One of a group of cells in the tongue that senses whether food is sweet, sour, salty, bitter, or savory.

Vein One of the vessels through which blood is sent back to the heart from other parts of the body.

Vibrate To move back and forth rapidly.

X-ray A picture of the inside of a person's body.